Paws for Thought

My Cat

CollinsPublishersSanFrancisco

A Division of HarperCollins*Publishers*

First published in 1996 by
Collins Publishers San Francisco
1160 Battery Street
San Francisco, CA 94111-1213
http://www.harpercollins.com

A Packaged Goods Incorporated Book

Conceived and produced by
Packaged Goods Incorporated
276 Fifth Avenue, New York, NY 10001
A Quarto Company

Project Director: Elizabeth Viscott Sullivan
Editor: Nichole T. Rustin
Designer: Tanya Ross-Hughes/HOTFOOT Studio
Illustrator: Christina Sun
Production: Tatiana Ginsberg and Amy Detjen

ISBN 0-00-225144-2

Color separations by Hong Kong Scanner
Printed in Hong Kong by Midas Printing Limited

CollinsPublishersSanFrancisco
A Division of HarperCollins*Publishers*

10 9 8 7 6 5 4 3 2 1

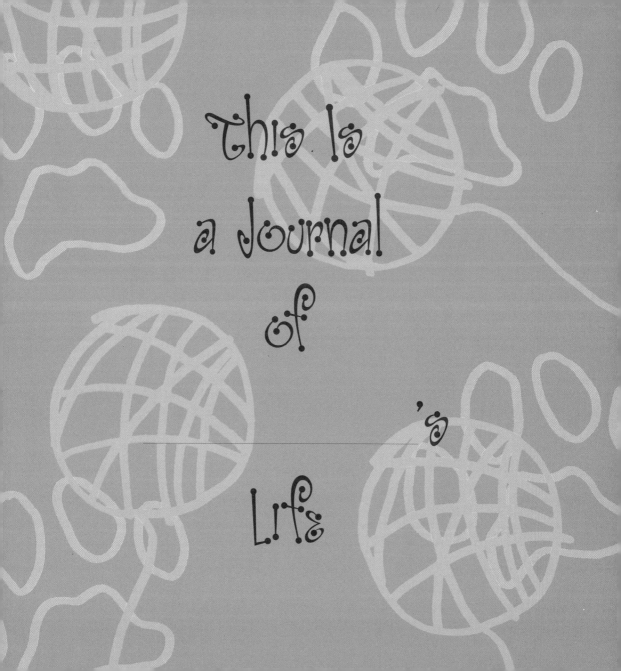

This Is
a Journal
of
_____'s
Life

Paw Print

DIRECTIONS: By using food coloring, which is harmless, you can make a print of your cat's paw. First, spread plenty of newspaper on the floor, then layer it with blank paper. Place your cat's paw into a flat dish containing the food coloring, then have it walk across the paper. After the coloring has dried, tape the final print onto this page.

My Cat

Name:
_____

Birthday:
_____

Place of birth:
_____

Registration number:
_____

Came to live with me on:
_____

Why I Chose My Cat

The smallest feline is a masterpiece. —Leonardo da Vinci

My Cat's Moving In

A Checklist

My Distinctive Cat

Breed: _____

Special markings (draw them in on the opposite page): _____

_____

Size: _____

Personality: _____

Habits: _____

Training My Cat

Growing up

My Cat's First Birthday

This Is No Ordinary Cat

Favorite Napping Places

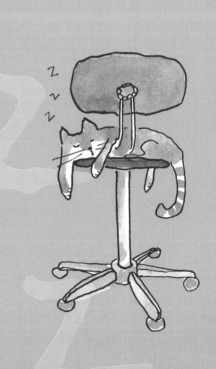

Favorite Toys

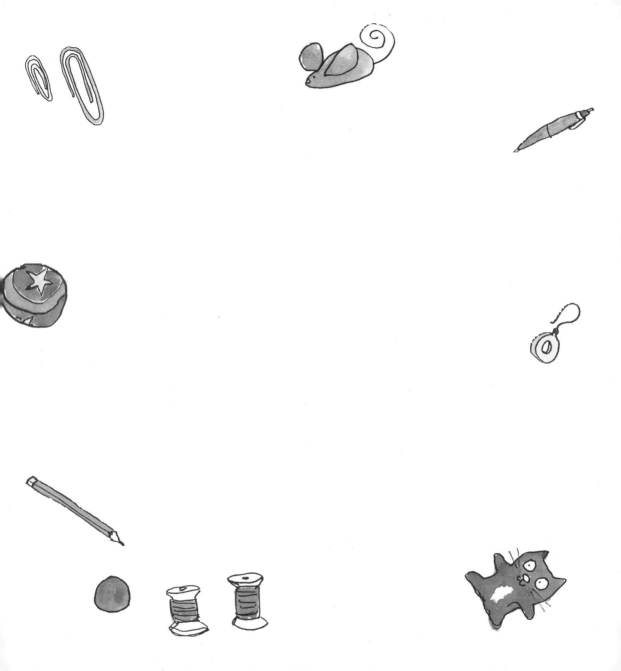

My Acrobatic Cat

lunge roll over

curl up LEAP

jump

flip

stretch run

POUNCE lunge

At the Vet

Veterinarian's name:

Address & phone number:

Date of visit:

Reason:

Recommendations:

Veterinarian's name:

Address & phone number:

Date of visit:

Reason:

Recommendations:

Veterinarian's name:

Address & phone number:

Date of visit:

Reason:

Recommendations:

Veterinarian's name:

Address & phone number:

Date of visit:

Reason:

Recommendations:

Veterinarian's name:

Address & phone number:

Date of visit:

Reason:

Recommendations:

Veterinarian's name:

Address & phone number:

Date of visit:

Reason:

Recommendations:

Age / Length / Weight

Age:

Length:

Weight:

Age:

Length:

Weight:

Age:

Length:

Weight:

Age:

Length:

Weight:

Age:

Length:

Weight:

Age:

Length:

Weight:

Medication Records

Vaccination: _____

Prescription: _____

Dosage: _____

Duration: _____

Reason: _____

_____

Vaccination: _____

Prescription: _____

Dosage: _____

Duration: _____

Reason: _____

_____

Vaccination:

Prescription:

Dosage:

Duration:

Reason:

Vaccination:

Prescription:

Dosage:

Duration:

Reason:

Vaccination:

Prescription:

Dosage:

Duration:

Reason:

Certificates and Documents

jump
curl up
roll over
flip
run
stretch
POUNCE

Cat Sitters

Name:
_____

Address:
_____

Availability:
_____

Instructions:
_____
_____

Name:
_____

Address:
_____

Availability:
_____

Instructions:
_____
_____

Name:
_____

Address:
_____

Availability:
_____

Instructions:
_____
_____

You may own a cat, but cannot govern one.   —Kate Sanborn

Favorite Foods

_____
_____
_____
_____
_____

Not So Favorite Foods

_____
_____
_____
_____
_____

My Cat & Me

If man could be crossed with the cat, it would improve man,
but it would deteriorate the cat. —Mark Twain

Favorite Places

Proud Moments

Crazy Times

On the Prowl

My Finicky Cat

Cats seem to go on the principle that it never does any harm
to ask for what you want. —Joseph Wood Kruich

My Cat's Territory

When We Play

When I play with my cat, who knows if she isn't amusing herself with me more than I am with her? —Michel de Montaigne

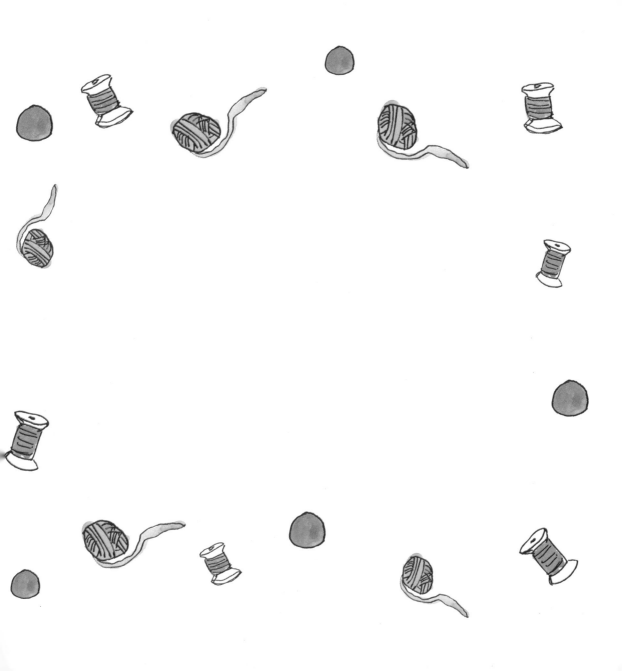

At the Groomer's

Cat Tales: The Memorable Adventures of _____

On the Road

Trips We've Taken, What We've Seen

My Cat Oughta Be in Pictures

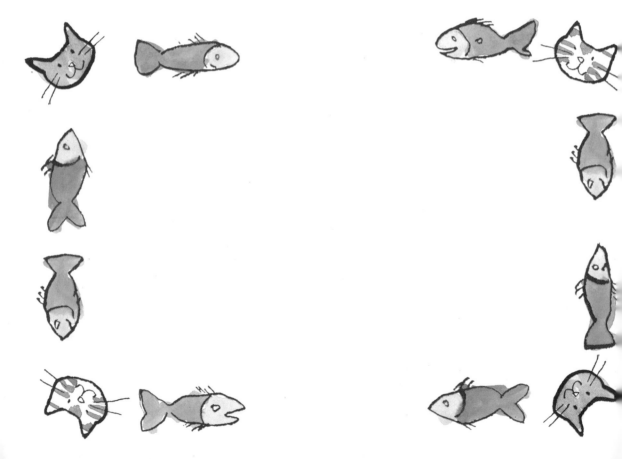

Friends & Foes

Before a cat will condescend to treat you like a trusted friend, some little token of esteem is needed, like a dish of cream.   —T.S. Eliot

Notes